Love Magic

*Ways to enhance your
love life and friendships using
the powers of magic & nature*

Antonia Beattie

BARNES
& NOBLE
BOOKS
NEW YORK

Contents

Love
Magic

Contents

Introduction —
Love Conquers All

Two human loves make one divine.
Elizabeth Barrett Browning

$\mathcal{L}$ove is one of the most powerful forms of energy known to us, whether it is the love of a mother for her child, a strong bond between lifelong friends or the hot, passionate love felt by young lovers. Its power has been commented on by philosophers and poets since ancient times, and is best expressed by a simple ancient Latin phrase — *Amor Omnia Vincit*, which translates as "Love Conquers All".

Although it might seem a rather simple concept, the influence of love is so universal that it profoundly affects every important aspect of life. From love, life itself springs forth. This is an underlying theme in Western mythology, in which the seasons progress through the year as a love story between the god, the symbol of male energy, and the goddess, the symbol of female energy. In Eastern philosophy, the image of yin/yang could really be used as a love symbol, denoting the blending of female and male energies, respectively.

The balance between male or extrovert energy and female or introvert energy is echoed in the balance of energies in the natural world — between the sun and the moon, summer and winter, and between fire and water. The Ancients believed that by understanding how to harmonize opposing aspects, human beings could achieve a true balance in their lives.

Many magicians, both in the East and the West, also believed in learning from the lessons of nature, because they understood that the chemistry of love is strongly related to the working of magic. Among other benefits, it was found that the energy produced by love could be harnessed to power the strongest of spells.

In modern times, love has been abused in a myriad of ways in a highly technological world where power is often based on an unnatural foundation. As human beings again search for meaning in their lives, the beauty, simplicity and sanctity of love is again becoming more and more evident.

Love magic is a way of harnessing the energy of love, and can be a beautiful and gentle way to reconnect with the balance of nature. This book blends the wisdom of ancient civilizations as those of China and India to understand the attracting and opposing forces that shape our lives, together with simple techniques which, if practiced in a heartfelt manner, can have the most beneficial effect on your life and those precious to you.

You have to love yourself before anyone else can love you. Learn to love yourself with honesty and carry this through to your love for others.

The Basics of Love Magic

What is love magic?

*Life begets life. Energy creates energy. It is by
spending oneself that one becomes rich.*
Sarah Bernhardt

*L*ove magic is a series of techniques or practices that help you achieve a sense of harmony within yourself and with your loved ones, which in turn enhances your ability to nurture and improve the quality of your relationships. There is no "right" way to practice love magic. In this book there are many ideas culled from a number of traditions, philosophies and cultures on how to incorporate the beauty of love magic into your life. It is up to you to tailor these ideas to your lifestyle and circumstances.

Traditionally, in Western magic, witches were often approached to work spells, brew potions and make amulets to attract lovers and friends. The spells that worked the best were often those that attracted compatible people to each other. In "white" witchcraft, the manipulation of people for inharmonious purposes was avoided at all costs because of ethical reasons and the magical backlash that invariably occurred.

In modern Western pagan movements and ancient Eastern sex magic traditions, the strong force of energy released at the climax of the sexual act was recognized as being one of the most powerful ways of gaining spiritual awakening. These are very powerful practices that are beyond the scope of this book.

However, aspects of how harmony can be achieved between human beings can be learned from the masters of the Indian tradition of Tantric yoga. They believed that to truly enjoy our relationships we must be in harmony with ourselves, each other and the rhythms of the natural world around and above us, such as the sun, moon and the planets. How to attain this sense of harmony and use it to heal or deepen our relationships is one of the most important purposes of this book.

How does it work with friends and lovers?

*Love does not consist in gazing at each other but looking
outward together in the same direction.*
Antoine de Saint-Exupery

Love magic can only be successfully practiced with your friends or
lover if you feel absolutely comfortable with them and if you are sure
that they are unconditionally open to deepening or improving their
relationship with you.

If you are involved in a tense relationship, do not worry. Practice
by yourself the techniques outlined in this book. This can create a
kind of force field around you that can trigger other people to relate
to you in a harmonious way. Be aware, however, that some people
feel so damaged by life that your growing sense of harmony may be
a source of great discomfort for them. If you possibly can, try to
allow these people to move out of your life or to have a lesser effect
on your emotions.

Although there is really no set path in practicing love magic,
consider incorporating the basics of good magical practices in the
following order:

- Find or create a special place where you can feel comfortable and
  safe for love magic practice (see pages 24–31).
- Concentrate on feeling the harmony within yourself (see pages
  32–39) and resolving hurt feelings or the feeling of being
  victimized (see pages 40–45).
- Practice love magic concerning yourself or anyone else with great
  care and love, whether you are using techniques to attract a new
  friend or lover (see pages 46–54) or for a specific purpose, such
  as strengthening your relationships (see page 56–65), or saying
  goodbye (see page 66–75).

Spellcraft — the Western tradition

A spell is a way of focusing the mind to help achieve a particular purpose. The key to spellcraft is to decide what you want. By the sheer act of concentration on what you wish, it could be said that you are opening an "astral doorway" to a new reality in which your desires will actually manifest.

To aid concentration, traditions have evolved over the centuries concerning what images or words are most effective for fulfilling certain goals, such as using red candles for a love spell. When you link into these traditions you can sometimes help the spell to work, because the procedures repeated over and over again seem to gradually build up their own energy.

To cast a spell successfully, you must not only believe that the spell can work, but also that you personally can make the change happen. Feeling empowered to make changes is one of the most important keys to successful spellcraft.

You must also think through the consequences of the spell. Love spells should be approached with caution. It is fine to ask for a glimpse at one's

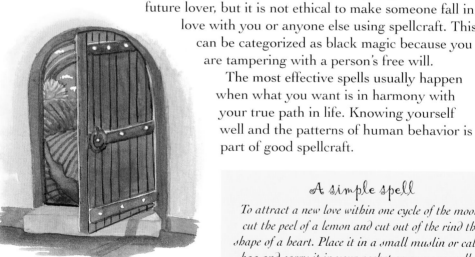

future lover, but it is not ethical to make someone fall in love with you or anyone else using spellcraft. This can be categorized as black magic because you are tampering with a person's free will.

The most effective spells usually happen when what you want is in harmony with your true path in life. Knowing yourself well and the patterns of human behavior is part of good spellcraft.

A simple spell

To attract a new love within one cycle of the moon, cut the peel of a lemon and cut out of the rind the shape of a heart. Place it in a small muslin or calico bag and carry it in your pocket or purse or wallet.

The power of the moon

In certain periods of history, such as the Renaissance period in the early 1500s, marriages and business contracts were only conducted during the phase of a new moon. The symbol of the new moon, the crescent, was thought to be lucky, a symbol of new promise and creation. Any new venture which occurred during the full moon was thought to be unlucky. Children born during a full moon were thought to be doomed to a life of ill health.

However, the full moon is also one of the most effective times to do any type of magic. It is believed that the fullness of the moon relates to a heightened level of spiritual energy that can be used for white magic.

Traditionally, spells were cast according to the phases of the moon. In many traditions during the waxing of the moon (when the moon is increasing), all positive spells were cast, such as love and healing spells. Negative spells, such as a spell dealing with the ending of things, were done during the waning of the moon (when the moon is decreasing).

Full moon is the time for most workings that involve healing, divination and the making of amulets and talismans for positive purposes such as the emotional protection of yourself or others. This is also a good time to balance any sense of inadequacy in yourself. The phase of a new moon is a perfect time to seek aid and guidance about a new project, relationship or career.

New moon spell

Pick some yarrow during new moon and sew it into a little linen or cotton bag. Place the bag under your pillow and say the following to find out who is your best friend:

"Thou pretty herb of Venus' tree
Thy true name it is yarrow
Now who my bosom friend may be
Pray tell thou me tomorrow."

The heavens and your astrological compatibility

The observation of the sun, moon and heavenly bodies and how their movements appear to correspond to various aspects of human life, including a person's love life and relationships, developed around 3000 B.C.

Astrology, believed to be one of humankind's earliest magical practices, revolved around the specific idea that there were 12 constellations through which the sun, moon and planets traveled. The Greeks, the Chinese, the Hindus and the Tibetans all developed their own form of astrology, and over the centuries astrologers began to see the relationship between a person's fate and the position of the heavenly bodies at his or her birth. The movement of the planets do not necessarily determine our inescapable fate, but indicate certain life patterns that can be tempered.

Each astrological sun sign also corresponds with an element such as earth, air, fire and water. Knowing how elements interact with each other is an important clue to how inherently compatible you are with your lovers, family and friends, for instance:

- Fire and air blend easily together so that those born under the astrological sun signs for fire and air are compatible.

- Earth and water do well together so that those born under the astrological sun signs for earth and water are also compatible.

Compatibility between fire and earth or air and earth or air and water or fire and water can be a bit more challenging and will require people to be much more understanding and tolerant of each other. For further compatibility concepts see pages 14–15.

Astrological chart of correspondences

Sun sign	Corresponding planet	Corresponding element	Sun sign	Corresponding planet	Corresponding element
Aries	Mars	Fire	Libra	Venus	Air
Taurus	Venus	Earth	Scorpio	Mars	Water
Gemini	Mercury	Air	Sagittarius	Jupiter	Fire
Cancer	Moon	Water	Capricorn	Saturn	Earth
Leo	Sun	Fire	Aquarius	Uranus	Air
Virgo	Mercury	Earth	Pisces	Neptune	Water

The chart below highlights the list of compatible sun signs. If you are an Aries, that is, born between 20 March and 20 April, look at the right hand column to see which sun signs are compatible to you. Check the left hand column to find out the birth dates for the particular sun signs.

Astrological compatibility chart

WHAT SUN SIGN ARE YOU?	WHO IS COMPATIBLE WITH YOU?
Aries March 20 to April 20	Friends: Gemini, Aquarius Lovers: Leo, Sagittarius
Taurus April 21 to May 21	Friends: Cancer, Pisces Lovers: Virgo, Capricorn
Gemini May 22 to June 21	Friends: Aries, Leo Lovers: Libra, Aquarius
Cancer June 22 to July 22	Friends: Taurus, Virgo Lovers: Scorpio, Pisces
Leo July 23 to August 23	Friends: Gemini, Libra Lovers: Aries, Sagittarius
Virgo August 24 to September 23	Friends: Cancer, Scorpio Lovers: Taurus, Capricorn
Libra September 24 to October 23	Friends: Leo, Sagittarius Lovers: Gemini, Aquarius
Scorpio October 24 to November 23	Friends: Virgo, Capricorn Lovers: Cancer, Pisces
Sagittarius November 24 to December 21	Friends: Libra, Aquarius Lovers: Aries, Leo
Capricorn December 22 to January 20	Friends: Scorpio, Pisces Lovers: Taurus, Virgo
Aquarius January 21 to February 18	Friends: Aries, Sagittarius Lovers: Gemini, Libra
Pisces February 19 to March 19	Friends: Taurus, Capricorn Lovers: Cancer, Scorpio

Compatibility and the elements

In Western magic and in the Ayurvedic medical traditions of India, five elements must be combined for successful magic workings and for healthy bodies — air, fire, water, earth and spirit (or ether, in India). It is believed that the elements represent important forces shaping the world and that the human biological system reflects the same forces at work in the body.

The Chinese believe that the year of a person's birth, when reduced in a certain way (see below) to a single digit, matches a particular element. Each single digit relates to one of the five Chinese elements. These elements, which differ slightly from the Western and Indian versions, are water, fire, wood, metal, earth. By understanding how the elements interact in the physical world, we can gain some surprising insights into how we interact among ourselves.

To tell which element corresponds to the year of your birth, add the last two digits of the year you were born and subtract that sum from the sum of the first two digits of your year of birth. For example, if you were born in 1963, you would do the following calculation:

$$1 + 9 = 10$$
$$10 - 9 = 1$$
$$6 + 3 = 9$$

Upon consulting the diagram on page 15, we see that number 1 relates to the water element. Repeat the exercise for your friends and lover and see which elements correspond to their years of birth. Now check the diagram on page 15 to see how your friends relate to you.

The energy of the circle, called the "Shen" cycle, indicates which elements support the other, for example, fire supports earth. Follow the arrows in a clockwise direction to find out the positive effect of the other elements.

The energy of the five-pointed star, called the "Ko" cycle, indicates which elements override the energy of another element, for example, wood tends to dominate earth. Follow the arrows of the star to find out the negative effect of the other elements.

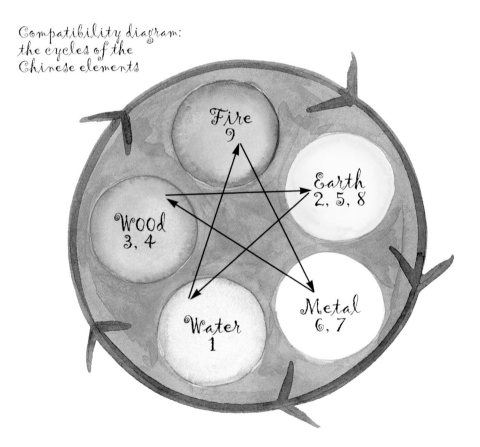

Compatibility diagram:
the cycles of the
Chinese elements

Fire
9

Earth
2, 5, 8

Wood
3, 4

Water
1

Metal
6, 7

The chakras — the flow of energy through your body

The chakras are a group of a number of energy centers running through the middle of your body. The Buddhists believe that there are seven chakras which correspond to the seven colors of the rainbow:

- base of the spine (red)
- the sacrum (just below the navel) (orange)
- the solar plexus (yellow)
- the heart (green)
- the throat (blue)
- the middle of the forehead (the "third eye") (purple)
- the top of the head (indigo)

An excellent technique to harmonize yourself with the rhythm of the earth is to visualize a stream or line of energy flowing from the earth through to the base of your spine "lighting up" a red glow at that point. Visualize the line of energy moving up your spine through each chakra and feel each area being "lit" with its appropriate color. Do this until you reach the top of your head. Allow the energy to flow from the top of your head back to the ground and then imagine the energy flowing back up your spine in a gentle loop.

Feel the energy flowing into the different chakras, clearing any fears or unhappy memories. It is believed that each chakra is attuned to different emotions. If you have some unhappiness about any experiences with past lovers, you may feel some tension in the sacrum, or if you have been unable to speak your feelings to someone you care about, you may find some difficulties imagining a light shining in the region of your throat. To finish the exercise, reverse the flow of the energy into the ground and allow the light in the chakras to dim.

Crown chakra

Third-eye chakra

Throat chakra

Heart chakra

Solar plexus chakra

Sacrum chakra

Base chakra

Attuning Your Senses to Use Love Magic

Using nature to enhance your relationships

*T*he smell and feel of certain herbs, flowers and stones can have an important effect on your sense of harmony. Consider working with the following natural objects and see which one/s appeal to you.

Herbs

Herbs have been used for love magic since time immemorial, particularly for a number of specific purposes, such as fertility and to promote visions.

Certain herbs can be burnt as an essential oil or kept as a bundle of dried herbs to add a certain atmosphere or to give you protection. Gather fresh herbs during the evening at the time of the waxing moon.

Magical herbs

Herb	Magical properties
Chamomile	*calming, protecting*
Cinnamon	*aids concentration and focus*
Frankincense	*protective, cleansing*
Garlic	*protective, strengthening*
Lavender	*increases awareness*
Lovage	*attracts romance*
Mistletoe	*protective, promotes harmony*
Sage	*enhances wisdom, cleanses evil*
Verbena	*enhances lucid dreaming*

Flowers

Flower magic is very sensitive and delicate, as you use cut flowers which have a fairly short life span. It is a magic that is developed according to your own reactions to the flower's scent. Choose the flowers that mean the most to you, maybe they remind you of a particular time or state of mind. Become familiar with those flowers and study their vibrations and what they mean to you. Some of the traditional meanings for flowers are found in the table opposite (top right). Feel free to make your own chart.

Flowers for Love Magic

Flowers	Properties
Cornflower	abundance, fertility
Jasmine	sensual love
Lavender	unresolved guilt
Red rose	passionate love
Sunflower	strength, courage, self-esteem
Tulip	strong bonds
Violets	comfort in times of sorrow
Water lily	love, calmness

Stones

To use the magic of precious and semi-precious stones, it is important to gather over a period of time the stones that speak to you about certain issues concerning your relationships. Keep a conscious thought in your mind about a certain issue, say the gaining of a new, supportive friend, before you go to choose a stone. For some people, the first stone they touch while focusing on the issue, will be the stone that represents that issue for them.

As you collect your stones, cleanse them with salt water or in a natural stream to remove any previous negative vibrations, then store them in a special box or basket, preferably lined with fabric, to keep them safe.

Stones and gems for Love Magic

Stone or gem	Magical properties
Agate	improves energy
Aquamarine	retains affection
Amethyst	enhances dreams
Beryl	facilitates favorable marriages
Bloodstone	relieves depression
Garnet	heightens sexuality
Jade	assists self-appreciation
Lapis lazuli	promotes success in love
Pearl	releases anger
Tourmaline	wins friends

Candle magic

Primarily, candle magic involves choosing a colored candle that will help you focus on what you wish to happen. Choose the color of your candle either according to your intuition or by choosing a color with the appropriate corresponding meaning from the table below.

Once you have chosen your candle, you will need to prepare it. First, choose an appropriate oil, such as patchouli oil for a red love candle, and rub the oil into the candle. This is called anointing the candle. Olive oil is a good substitute if you do not have access to aromatherapy oils.

Consider carving a simple word to sum up your wish down the side of the candle.

When ready, place your candle onto or into a safe receptacle, such as a small bowl half filled with sand to catch the falling wax. Sit in front of your prepared candle and imagine a blue circle vibrating around you. This circle of light will provide you with a sense of protection from any interruptions and ill thoughts.

Color of candle	Corresponding meaning
Red	*sexual love, high energy*
Pink	*affectionate love*
Orange	*openness, flexibility*
Yellow/gold	*confidence, charm*
Blue	*patience, calm*

Once you are feeling safe, look into the flame and visualize the successful outcome of your wish. Do not allow any undermining messages to dwell in your mind. Let these disruptive thoughts float away and continue your concentration until you feel ready to extinguish the candle. Put out your candle and watch the smoke rise from the wick, imagining that your spell is intermingling with reality, already changing your life according to your wishes.

Intimacy and food — the ingredients of love

Since ancient times certain foods, such as oysters, caviar and chocolate, have been used to add spice to a person's love life.

What is so special about these foods? All foods contain energy, which has a range of influences on the chemistry of our body. In Chinese medicine, salty foods such as caviar have a yang energy, meaning that the energy is warming, active and stimulating to the chakras in the lower part of the spine. Sugary foods, such as chocolate, have a yin energy, meaning that the energy is cooling, passive and affects the chakras in the upper body, from the heart to the crown (see page 16–17). Salty, warming foods can be used between lovers, while sugary treats would be appropriate for showing your loved ones affection.

The traditions concerning the sharing of food are also fundamental to love magic. The action of "breaking bread" with a person is in itself a silent signal of friendship and trust. You are trusting that the person you invite into your home will not harm you and your visitor is trusting that you will not poison him or her. In love magic, your visitor should not be subjected to subtle attempts through food to make him or her fall in love with you. Do not tamper with a person's free will. Rather, make a free sharing of your food and nurturing or better still, share in the preparation of a meal.

Love foods

Apple	Chocolate	Pineapple
Avocado	Ginger	Pistachio
Banana	Hazelnuts	Raspberries
Brazil nuts	Lavender	Rose
Cardamom	Mango	Strawberries
Cinnamon	Orange	Vanilla
Clove	Passionfruit	
Cherry	Peaches	

Another use for hazelnuts

In Roman times, it was traditional to throw hazelnuts at a newly wed couple instead of the rice or confetti that we use in modern times.

The sensuality of fabrics

Do you remember having, or do you now have a dress, shirt, robe or other garment that made you feel good, as if nothing could touch you? A garment that you would pull out of the wardrobe when you needed that extra burst of confidence? Taking notice of what makes a fabric or garment special to you is useful in developing some personal tools that help interweave love magic into your life.

For any exercises that involve helping you feel better about yourself, it may be useful to have something that acts like a magic robe. See if you can find or, better still, make your own magic robe. For those of you who sew, your magic robe could be anything from a bath robe, through an oversize dress to a theatrical cape with a hood. You can incorporate beads, tassels and secret pockets into your own design or a store-bought pattern. It is an excellent gift for yourself and is a wonderful gift idea for a loved one.

It is important that your magic robe is comfortable and fairly loose. Try to have your robe made from natural fibers, such as silk, cotton, linen, wool or even hemp. These fabrics allow your skin to breathe. Be generous with the quantity of cloth so you can feel enfolded in the fabric, and enjoy the sensation as it caresses your skin.

Keep your garment only for special occasions, when you are with your love or talking into the night with a close friend or when you are doing any of the exercises in this book.

Never give a knife or a pair of scissors as a gift unless the recipient of the gift gives you a coin. Knives and scissors were thought to be able to cut the cord of friendship.

The secret language of colors — auras

The use of colors in love magic is a fascinating one. The seven rainbow colors that make up the spectrum of light each have their own vibrations that can resonate with other vibrations or energy forms, such as the seven chakras, musical tones and even the planets. Auras are vibrations emanating from our body and head in waves of color, and with a little practice we can see the aura around our friends and loved ones.

It is easiest to concentrate on trying to see the nimbus, the head aura. Have your subject stand in front of either a dark or completely white background. Concentrate on the middle of the forehead, an area called the third eye. You may start to fancy that you see some color around the head. Do not look directly at the color but keep it within your peripheral vision. As you get used to seeing the aura, you will eventually be able to study how much energy your subject has. As a general rule of thumb, if the aura is close to the head, your friend or lover is very low in energy. If the aura is expansive, the energy level is high.

Visualizing color around your subject, or chanting a certain tone that resonates with the magical purpose of the color, can help enormously in revitalizing your subject's vitality. Pick the appropriate color from the chart below and experiment. Feel free to develop your own chart.

Color	Love Magic Purpose	Tone
Red	*stimulates energy flow*	A
Orange	*allows easy communication*	B
Yellow	*uplifts*	D
Green	*soothes an aching heart*	E
Blue	*calms*	F
Indigo	*eases emotional fears*	C
Purple	*facilitates spiritual love*	G

Creating a Special Space

The importance of having your own special space

*L*ove magic can be one of the most challenging types of magic that you can attempt since it requires you to examine how you see yourself and your relationships with other people. This can lead to a feeling of vulnerability. To offset this, it is important to establish a special protective space for yourself, in either your home or garden, that can serve as a special retreat. You can use your retreat to practice exercises suggested in this book, such as the important "grounding" which you can do if you are feeling unhappy or unfocused.

Unhappiness or the inability to focus can be a symptom that your energies are too scattered or that you are rundown. Often a state of panic is experienced, and there is sometimes a feeling of victimization or of things being out of control. You cannot do any successful magic feeling like this. However, once you have your special place set up, you will be able to revitalize quietly by linking back to the earth and your own body.

To bring your energies back into your body, take your favorite crystal or stone (such as ironstone or hematite) and push it into the earth or floorboards, imagining that your energy is flowing down through your body into the earth. Imagine that you are being given another current of strong, fresh energy from the earth that passes through the stone .

Another way to ground yourself is to visualize yourself as a tree. Concentrate on your spine as you are sitting comfortably, and imagine that your spine is illuminated in an iridescent green light, like the colors you sometimes see on the wings of a beetle. Then turn that light into the trunk of a tree. Imagine the base of your tree trunk extending downward into the earth and watch the roots grow and spread, stabilizing your body as they deepen, drawing energy up from the earth.

Choosing a special space

You will need to find a private space either in nature or indoors where you can practice love magic or simply revitalize without distractions or interruptions, away from everyday life. Consider the spare room, the loft, or even look at converting the garden shed. Let your intuition be your guide.

If you live in the country, you may already know of a place to which you feel particularly attuned. Evaluate the safety of your area, if it is outdoors, and make sure it is free from distractions.

If you live in the city, you may be lucky enough to be able to set aside a small room for your sacred place. It is surprising how soon a room like this becomes the heart of your home and how it helps you attune with nature despite the city noise around you. Alternatively, you may wish to set up your space near where you dream.

You may wish to set up a small collection of objects, pictures and candles, honoring yourself, your friends, your loved one or your relationship together. In feng shui, the ancient Chinese art of design and placement, special places in your home are considered lucky for relationships and useful friends. When standing just inside your front door, the section of your house to the right of your front door is considered, if using the bagua, to be a lucky spot for useful friends and travel, while the section of your house toward the back on the right hand side is particularly important concerning your lover and other close relationships. Use these spots in your home to pay homage to your relationships by assembling the objects and pictures that promote harmony and a remembrance of the happiness you have shared together.

The Feng Shui bagua grid

Wealth	Fame	Relationships
Background Information	Health	New projects
Inner wisdom	Career/ lifestyle	Help from people

Making a space feel safe

To strengthen the feeling of protection that your safe space should provide, consider "casting" a circle to protect against interruptions and harmful thoughts. The circle is a very powerful sign, symbolizing infinity, unity and the cycle of the seasons. It is advisable to conduct any love magic spells or exercises within a circle.

To create a circle is to create a safe space in which you can link yourself into the earth before using your space as a doorway to your higher self. A circle is thought to be a space between the worlds, a space from which it is possible to direct your psychic energy.

Before you cast your circle you first need to purify your body and your space. For your own purification, it is an agreeable idea to have a ritual bath perfumed with your favorite oil and lit by a single candle. After bathing, gather all the things you need to cast a spell or perform an exercise and bring them into your special place. Wear something comfortable and loose, preferably your special garment (see page 22).

Back at your special place, sprinkle salt around your circle perimeter, walking deosil (clockwise in the northern hemisphere and counter-clockwise in the southern hemisphere). When you are ready, sit quietly in your circle and visualize a line of blue light circling around you, then imagine the circle growing into a sphere. Your space is now protected until you finish your working. To move back into the real world, imagine the blue sphere reabsorbed by the earth, and take time to ground yourself (see page 24).

The Wedding Ring

Wedding rings symbolized a magic circle made around the couple, containing the happiness of their union.

The bedroom

To prepare your bedroom for love magic practices or exercises, consider setting up a special section on your dressing table, bookshelf or special table in your bedroom to honor your lover and your love together.

As part of your decoration of this specially dedicated table, it is important to collect images or objects that represent the four elements — earth, air, fire and water. For the proper flow of psychic energy you must pay attention to a balanced combination of the four elements. You will need:

- a crystal or stone ball to symbolize EARTH;
- incense, oil burner and/or fresh flowers (preferably white) to symbolize AIR;
- a wooden branch or candles to symbolize FIRE;
- a pair of wine goblets to symbolize WATER.

If possible, place your table against the corner to the right and on the wall opposite the entrance to your bedroom. In feng shui, using the bagua, this is the optimum spot for relationships. Also add pictures, preferably framed in gold or silver, of your lover and yourself together. Use your imagination and be guided by your intuition as to any other additions to your table.

The bath tub

The bathroom is traditionally a place of purification. Having a bath before you enter your special place and doing any of the love magic exercises or spells is a very effective way of clearing away all the troubles of the day prior to doing some psychic work.

If you are having your bath in the evening, choose a beeswax candle, and place it where you can gaze at it while you are bathing. Use a drop or two of an essential oil in your bath water, mixing it through the water thoroughly, and bring with you a large glass of cool water.

As you soak in your bath, take notice of all your senses. Check the taste in your mouth, taking a sip of water to cleanse your palate if necessary. Notice the scent of the oils you have chosen, create little waves in your tub with your hands, listen to the motion of the water and feel how it caresses your skin.

Allow your eyes to stare momentarily at the lighted candle. Close your eyes and imagine the candle flame in the middle of your forehead, your "third" eye. Hold the image for as long as possible and then relax with your eyes closed, visualizing any stray thoughts of the day encapsulated in a bubble floating away from you. When ready, get out of the bath, dry yourself with a fresh towel and let the water out, watching the water and all your worries go down the drain. As a variation, and if your bath tub or spa allows, you may vary this exercise by practicing it with your loved one.

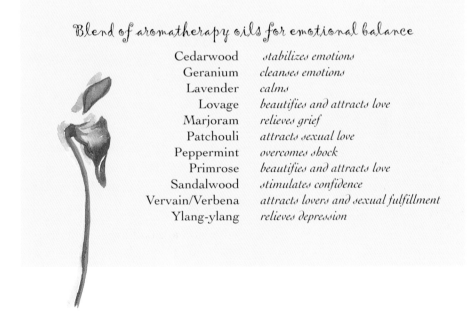

Blend of aromatherapy oils for emotional balance

Cedarwood	*stabilizes emotions*
Geranium	*cleanses emotions*
Lavender	*calms*
Lovage	*beautifies and attracts love*
Marjoram	*relieves grief*
Patchouli	*attracts sexual love*
Peppermint	*overcomes shock*
Primrose	*beautifies and attracts love*
Sandalwood	*stimulates confidence*
Vervain/Verbena	*attracts lovers and sexual fulfillment*
Ylang-ylang	*relieves depression*

Before the fireplace

Traditionally the element of fire symbolizes your will. Often our inability to exercise our will can be due to overpowering emotional unhappiness of one sort or another. Consider using fire to burn away any emotions that are holding you back from expressing yourself or from having happy relationships, such as fear or what other people might think or the fear of failure or disappointment.

   If you have a working fireplace in your home, gather together wood, fire starters, matches, some comfortable cushions, paper and your favorite pen. Sit comfortably after lighting your fire and watch the flames. Allow your mind to focus on what is undermining your will, particularly examining what fears block your path.

   When ready, write down your fear on a large sheet of paper no less than standard letter size — if you have more than one fear repeat this process at another time. Fold the piece of paper four times and throw it onto the fire. Watch the flames ignite the paper (symbolizing the illumination you have had in identifying the fear) and watch the folded paper shrivel up in the heat of the flame (symbolizing your will conquering the fear). Continue watching the flames consume your fear to

nothing and observe the smoke rising up the chimney away from you.

   After having done this exercise by yourself, you may wish to share the practice with your lover or friend so that both of you can burn a shared fear that is troubling your relationship. However, take it gently and establish your boundaries if either of you feel uncomfortable.

   Even if you do not have a fireplace, you can still do this exercise by using a large bowl or copper cauldron half filled with enough sand to contain a small fire.

In the outdoors — how does your garden grow?

There is an ancient belief in India that the state of your mind and body can be compared to a garden. You can learn some surprising things from seeing yourself as a garden. Sit or lie comfortably in your special place. Close your eyes and focus your mind on the image of a garden. Imagine walking into it. Use all your senses to describe your garden to yourself, for example:

- What does it look like?
- Is it well tended?
- Is there a pleasant scent in the air?
- Do the plants look and feel healthy and happy?
- Can you hear any birds or rustlings in your garden?
- Is there fruit in your garden? If so, how does it taste?

The answer to these questions can give you a good indication of how you are faring within your body and spirit. Check to see whether your garden has a boundary. If the boundary is too close, you may be dealing with issues of being too confined in your life. If you cannot see the boundaries, you may be suffering from having your energies too thinly spread. If the fence along the boundary is in poor repair, you may have suffered from people trying to invade your personal space.

To help rectify the situation in real life, it is sometimes useful to do this visualization and imagine yourself removing the weeds, rebuilding the fence or planting beautiful plants in your garden.

If your special space is outside in your garden, make sure to "cleanse" the area first by sprinkling some salt and water around the perimeter of your area.

31

Feeling magical

Accepting your body

One of the most important issues to address in relation to love magic is your ability to accept and trust your senses, your feelings and your body. Your senses and attuning them to love magic is discussed on pages 18–23. It is only when you are comfortable with yourself, can you truly relate to other people in your relationships. Only then will you relate to another person on equal terms.

In magical terms, your own feelings and beliefs about yourself create a particular form of energy. It is this energy field that people sense or are attracted to. You must remember that the type of energy you project is to a great extent your own choice. This is an important part of magic — belief in yourself.

Sometimes our energy flags and all of a sudden we can feel ugly, stupid or physically unattractive. For many there is the temptation to counter such feelings by reaching for sugar and junk food.

Stop for a moment and allow yourself to feel compassion for your body, allowing it to have a rest. Try the relaxation techniques on pages 34–35 and progress to the gentle but powerful exercises to help you find again your true self-worth (see pages 40–45). If you have been feeling down for a while, try a bit of mirror magic, described opposite.

Using mirror magic

Mirror magic is a very powerful way of helping boost your self-confidence and self-esteem. Although it may seem very challenging to some, it is a remarkably easy exercise to practice after the first try.

All you need is a full-length mirror which you can set up in your special space. Allow yourself at least an hour to fully relax into the exercise. You may dress in your special garment (see page 22) or, for a particularly powerful effect, consider doing this exercise naked.

When ready, stand in front of the mirror, and become aware of the sensations of your body. Check particularly how your back feels. If your lower back feels a little strain while standing, tilt your pelvis forward. You will find that your knees will unlock and bend slightly and that standing for any length of time will be easier.

Look at yourself in the mirror. Try to distance yourself from your old reactions of yourself by merely concentrating on your breathing. Now feel the energy in your feet sinking through the floor down to the earth. You may begin to feel a deep connection to the earth (the earth element is a symbol of the body), even a sense of increased stability and, finally, a powerful sense of tranquillity. Keep looking at yourself with this new feeling of quietness.

As an advanced exercise, have your friend or lover give you a big hug from behind as you are looking at yourself in the mirror. Absorb the mingling of acceptance from both yourself and your partner.

Relaxation techniques

Being relaxed is important for the practice of love magic. Being tense tends to inhibit your intuition and can cloud your judgments about people or yourself. Relaxation is an essential practice to incorporate into your life and one that may provide many long-term benefits.

Set up a comfortable mat on the floor for you to lie on in your special space. Make sure that you are warm enough. Always have a blanket near you if you feel cold, and have a pillow for your knees if lying on the floor upsets your lower back. Lie on your mat and close your eyes.

Imagine that you are walking down a flight of curved stone stairs, gently spiraling down to the next landing. There are nine steps in total. As you go down the stairs, feel that you are leaving your conscious world behind with each step. As you reach the landing you notice that your body feels totally quiet.

At the landing you find a great oak door with mystical symbols carved into the dark wood. Open the door and walk into a deeply colored, richly decorated hall. At the other end of the hall, you see a beautiful woman or man sitting on a throne. You are beckoned toward the throne and, as you approach, you feel a wave of complete acceptance and love emanating from this being.

When you reach the throne, you are invited to sit on it. The being stands behind the throne and places her or his hands on your shoulders. You feel a profound sense of support and compassion flowing from the being's hands into your body.

Stay in this state of relaxation for as long as you feel comfortable. When you are ready to go back to the ordinary world, stand up from your throne, thank the being for her or his support and walk back to the landing through the oak door. Before you close the oak door, turn and make a small, respectful bow to this being. As you begin to climb up the nine stairs, you will become more and more conscious of the ordinary world around you. Wriggle your toes and give your body a good stretch. As you reach the ninth step, open your eyes.

You should feel invigorated and deeply relaxed. Try this exercise every second day for a week, choosing a time when you know you will not be disturbed. For variety, you may wish to make your own script for your relaxation exercise.

Transforming your breath into magical energy

Magical practices are designed to heighten the level of energy in our bodies and to allow us insights into the use of this energy. Even how you breathe can affect the state of your conscious mind. Breath control is a powerful form of magic which can be incorporated into the art of love magic.

Try the following exercises that focus on breathing through the pores of the skin over the entire body. These exercises, for obvious reasons, are best practiced naked or in a minimum of clothing. Again set up a mat or a comfortable chair in your special space and imagine that with each breath you take, your body is filling with healing energy through the pores of the skin. With each breath you breathe out, imagine that your body is expelling unwanted energy through its pores.

Imagine the healing energy as a color. Work your way through the rainbow to see which colors appeal to you. You may find that the color will change from day to day, according to your mood. As an advanced exercise, practice breathing through the pores of certain sections of your body. Imagine your breath traveling to your hand, the chakra centers that run through the trunk of your body, or to an area in your body that is feeling constricted or ill at ease. If you are suffering from heartache, try breathing a calm green light through the pores of your chest.

The next stage to achieve is to transform the indrawn breath into a specific type of energy. This is useful for spell magic. You may wish to cast a protective spell. Imagine your inhalation being a gentle blue shade. The blue signifies harmonization with your intention — in this case, the protection of, say, your friend or lover. Imagine this blue breath mingling with your intention and then, with the next exhalation, feel that your breath and your intention are a particular type of energy force.

For a love magic spell, focus your breath into your hands. As you inhale imagine your breath turning into an energy suitable for the spell. If you are working a spell for your friend, imagine the indrawn breath turning a pale pink color. If you are working a spell for your lover, imagine the breath turning fire red in color. As you exhale, feel the breath and its heat coming through your hands as you use them to prepare the ingredients of the spell, and send its power out into the ether.

Awakening the senses — the art of self-massage

Self-massage is an excellent way to nurture yourself and to accept your body as it is. Imagine that you are sculpting your body into your desired form. The advantages of self-massage are many, ranging from improving the circulation to toning up your muscles. However, it is important to skip the self-massage for a day or so if you are suffering from a cold, fever or other severe health problem.

In Ayurvedic medicine, a system of medicine that originated in India many thousands of years ago, a practice of daily massage called abhyanga is recommended by Ayurvedic practitioners. Massaging your body and face can add an extra glow to your skin and increase your energy levels.

For a facial massage, use jojoba or almond oil which has been warmed in your hands, and apply it to your face with gentle but firm fingers. Massage the contours of your face, starting from the middle of your face and following the line of your eyebrows, sinus passages and chin to the side of your face. Use both hands to perform the action on both sides of your face at the same time. When you have finished your massage, allow the oil to stay on your face for at least five minutes then wash it off with cool, running water. Consider doing this simple exercise both morning and evening.

Facial recipe

For your facial massage, try the following recipe to further cleanse your skin:

1 cup jojoba or almond oil
1 cup glycerin (vegetable if possible)
10 drops tea tree oil
2 teaspoons of fresh lemon juice

Mix the ingredients together and keep in a tinted glass jar. Use one or two teaspoons of the facial cleanser with 1 fl. oz. (30 ml) of warm water and splash the diluted mixture on your face, massaging your skin as described above. Wash off with cool, running water.

For your body massage, use sesame oil which has been warmed in the cup of your hands. Do this exercise before your shower. In Ayurvedic medicine there is a particular sequence to be observed regarding which body part is massaged first.

Start with your heart and breasts, massaging the area over the heart in a clockwise circular motion and your right breast in a counterclockwise circular motion. Move to your stomach and massage that area with a clockwise circular motion. Move to your shoulders and massage them in long straight strokes, moving away from the neck. Massage your neck with short straight downward strokes and then massage each arm, stroking from the shoulders down to your hands. Next massage your hips, lower back and buttocks in a circular motion. Stroke your legs down to your feet and finish your massage with small circular motions on the tops and soles of your feet.

If you suffer from varicose veins or have a bruised area, avoid massaging that part of your body. Once you have finished your massage, leave the oil on your skin for at least five or ten minutes and then wash your body in the shower.

Emotional Healing

Getting in touch with your feelings

Sometimes past trauma or a lifestyle focused exclusively around work leads us to feel disjointed and as if we are not in control of our own life. The claims of work and difficult relationships can cause us to lose touch with our real feelings. How do we get back in touch with our feelings in the face of what seems to be overwhelming demands?

One effective way of coping with overpowering emotional crises, either past or present, is to focus your attention on what you are actually feeling. An excellent way of doing this is to start a journal. There are many journals available commercially that are a pleasure to hold or which are suitable for you to decorate.

Consider implementing a ritual of writing how you feel in your journal each evening. Always write what is true for you. Sit in your special space so that you can feel protected. If you are feeling particularly jittery, imagine a line of blue light running around you, keeping you safe from distractions and any unhappy feelings projected toward you by your friends or lover.

Implement this nightly ritual for yourself, particularly if you are experiencing a troublesome time. If you don't have the time to write each night, try to make a time at least once a week, on the same night or day and at the same time.

Ancient Wisdom
Try not to merely react in the moment. Pull back from the situation.
Take a wider view; compose yourself.
Epictetus, *The Art of Living* (55 A.D. — 135 A.D.)

Cleansing hurt feelings, guilt and pain

Often the hurt, guilt or pain we experience in our early years program a way of thinking or feeling that can undermine our self-confidence and self-esteem.

There are a number of techniques with which you can experiment to help you cleanse these feelings from your life. Once you can clear these undermining energies, you will find that you are able to focus on your will and get what you want from life.

The first step is to do a short meditation on what you are feeling. Always focus on your own feelings and not on the person you feel "caused" you to feel hurt, guilt or pain. There is a school of thought, going back to ancient Roman times, that it is your response to a person's emotional abuse that injures you rather than the abuse itself. The idea is that you are in fact free to choose to ignore that person's comments.

Isolate one specific feeling that is worrying you at the moment. Concentrate on that feeling. Allow the other issues to fade away — you can work on them in another session. As you are focusing on your feeling of hurt, guilt or pain, imagine that emotion being contained in a sphere. Allow the sphere to move out of your body and see it spinning gently in front of you at heart level.

As the sphere spins, imagine it being suffused with a particular color. Blue or green is always a good choice, as they are colors of healing. Imagine the sphere getting smaller and smaller until you can no longer see it. By reducing the sphere "containing" your particular feeling to nothing, a similar effect should be felt in relation to your emotions.

Ancient Myth

Since ancient times, mint has been used to temper anger, jealousy, and other high emotions. In Greek mythology, Persephone, the wife of Pluto, cools her husband's lust for a nymph by turning her into a mint bush.

Moon healing to release stress

Stress is another hindrance to the practice of love magic. We are continually subjected to stress in our ordinary world but there are a number of effective ways of releasing stress magically, particularly by using the powers of a full moon.

For the following exercise you will need:

- a bowl of water (preferably the bowl should be silver colored, such as stainless steel, to echo the shape of the full moon); and
- a piece of clear quartz crystal (choose a piece that is tumbled [polished] so that it is pleasantly smooth to your touch).

This exercise must be done in the evening under the light of a full moon. You may need to do this exercise outside or with the window open in your special space so that the moon's rays are shining onto your chosen area.

Prepare your tools. Make sure your bowl is washed and polished and that the water is fresh. Spring water is ideal. Place your stone under running water to remove any previous energy.

When ready, place your bowl of water on the moonlit floor or ground. Wash your stone, channeling all your feelings of stress into it. Imagine that the water and the moon's rays are cleansing the stress out of the stone. Continue until you feel calm and relaxed. Dry your stone and pour the water into the earth. Sit awhile, holding your stone, enjoying a release from your worries. Carry the stone with you during the day and rub it when you begin to feel any further stress. The moon's power, now contained in the stone, will help relieve your anxiety.

Moon magic

Sometimes those who do not feel that they have anything to give will feel that it is impossible to share their possessions or emotions. Watch the waxing and waning of the moon. Nature works in cycles. It is important to realize that, although we may feel at the ebb of our energy, the cycle will change and we will be able to feel the energy rise again. Try not to focus solely on the times when you have felt low. Like the moon, there will be times when you only wish to share a little bit of yourself and times when you are glowing brightly.

Balancing the elements — finding the Philosopher's Stone

In Chinese and Indian Ayurvedic medicine, there is a strong belief that the elements make up the world as well as our bodies. In Western magic, the elements are the cornerstone of all magical practices because they are believed to be the basis of all life.

In the Renaissance period, it was believed that the greatest magical prize, the Philosopher's Stone, was obtained when the elements were combined in the right proportions. The Philosopher's Stone meant many things to many people. Essentially it could do anything you wanted it to do, such as cure illnesses or change base metal into gold. In Ayurvedic medicine, it is believed that by harmonizing the elements in your body, you can achieve the best of health.

We can also seek emotional balance by uniting the elements. Since the Middle Ages, Western culture has ascribed certain personality traits to the four elements.

Element	Positive personality trait	Negative personality trait
Air	intellectual, social	irresponsible, unfeeling
Fire	courageous, active	angry, intolerant
Water	sensitive, receptive	unstable, jealous, possessive
Earth	practical, patient	restricted, unimaginative

Often the people we choose as friends provide an elemental personality that balances the element/s that are missing in our own personality. Check the table above to see which elements are strong in your own personality makeup. To attain a balance in your life, experiment with what it would take to incorporate into your life the positive personality traits of the other elements.

Creating an element chart will help you see which elemental characteristics are strong or weak in your life. Draw a circle and quarter it. Label each quarter as an element, starting from the top left hand side. Include other personality traits that you feel suit the elements. Look at what elements your friends and lover represent. This may provide you with invaluable insight as to the dynamics of your relationships.

Giving yourself permission to feel strong

If you feel a victim of circumstance and that you are being pushed around, it is important to allow your mind to make a mental shift about your situation.

Experiment with thinking that, rather than being helpless, you are allowing yourself to be downtrodden and that you do not have to continue doing so if you don't want to. Give yourself permission to feel that you are strong, that you are able to control many aspects of your life, particularly your way of thinking.

Use your mind to call up past scenarios in which you have felt victimized. Reconstruct those events as if you were strong and in control of the situation. What would you do? How would you feel? Slowly implement your newfound insight into practice in real-life situations. Sometimes, as you change your own perception of yourself, others intuitively follow your lead.

Keep in mind that strength must be balanced with wisdom. Such wisdom comes from watching and listening to the ordinary and spiritual worlds around you. You must always use your strength wisely.

Ancient Wisdom
Never depend on the admiration of others. There is no strength in it.
Epictetus, *The Art of Living* (55 A.D. — 135 A.D.)

Empowering your intuition through water scrying

One of the most intriguing ways of empowering your intuition is scrying. Scrying is a form of divination which interprets pictures, both moving or static, that appear to form through a mist in a crystal ball or in the smoke swirling inside a cauldron. It is no longer generally believed that the visions that are seen from scrying are messages from spirits or the devil. For some, scrying is a way of linking into their higher consciousness.

There are many forms of scrying. Crystal scrying requires a flawless quartz crystal ball. Use jasmine to charge its energy. Stones like the green-colored beryl is thought to be a particularly reliable stone for scrying.

Thick, plastic colorless balls are a cheaper alternative but have the disadvantage of being easy to scratch and are not so reliable. Scrying can also be done with a bowl of water and a good measure of black ink or, if you have a fireplace, it can be done by watching the flames rise and swirl above the crackling logs. As water is the element for emotions, try any scrying concerning your relationships with the bowl of water and some ink (say a tablespoon, depending on the size of your bowl). You will also most probably need to practice in quiet for at least a week before you start to see anything in the water.

The first step is to sit with your mind blank in front of the bowl of water. When you feel ready pour in a small amount of ink and gaze, not stare, into the water. Eventually shapes and patterns will emerge, revealing a picture. At first you will not have much control over what you see but as you progress you will be able to set questions in your mind, and allow the water to provide the answer visually. Your next step will be to interpret the pictures that you see — you may seek enlightenment from set dream symbols or from your own dream journal.

Scrying requires a great deal of concentration and you may wish to use an appropriate incense to help you focus, such as myrrh or peppermint.

Attracting a New Friend or Lover

Spells

A spell is a way of focusing your mind to achieve a particular purpose. There are two important elements to spellcraft.

First, you must decide what you want. Be careful what you ask for. Do not be tempted to tamper with another person's free will — this is getting close to black magic.

Many traditional spells were aimed at making another person fall in love with the magician or witch, irrespective of the intended lover's will, or to conjure spirits to coerce the girl/boy to come to the magician or witch. However, many magicians and witches paid a heavy price for such coercive behavior, including death. See pages 54 for the appropriate magical ethics which must be observed.

Today, the love spells you can ethically perform are those that relate to you and your feelings. Love spells to attract a new friend or lover into your life (with the exception of a specific person) are appropriate and are some of the most powerful spells there are.

Second, to help you achieve your will, you will need to learn the art of concentration. It could be said that, by the sheer act of concentration on what you wish, you are tuning into a new reality in which you may re-order various aspects of your life in the knowledge that these changes will be reflected in the everyday world.

Many spells are devised so that you collect specific images and objects or say words that help you concentrate on your purpose. Over the centuries, traditions have evolved concerning what images or words are most effective for fulfilling certain goals, such as using red candles for a love spell. It is always best to use materials that are as close to nature as possible, such as cotton, silk and beeswax, rather than artificial materials, because they are able to hold psychic energy more effectively.

The spells discussed in this book are devised to intensify your energy levels so that a beacon is virtually "switched on" to attract the right person

Type of attraction spell	Tools required	Timing and symbol
Influential mentor	*Orange non-drip candle,* *One drop of cinnamon, clove,* *sandalwood and/or orange.* *Magician card from a Tarot deck.*	*Day: Wednesday* *Symbol for Mercury:* ☿
True friend	*Blue non-drip candle,* *One drop of cedarwood. with* *a pinch of nutmeg.* *Ace of Cups card from a* *Tarot deck.*	*Day: Thursday* *Symbol for Jupiter:* ♃
Soul mate	*Rose colored non-drip candle.* *One drop of patchouli, rose,* *jasmine, mugwort and/or* *ylang-ylang.* *Lovers card from a Tarot deck.*	*Day: Friday* *Symbol for Venus:* ♀

to you, as either an influential mentor, a true friend or your soul mate.

The spells using these ingredients should be cast during the waxing of the moon on the relevant day and in the third hour after sunset. Inscribe the appropriate planetary image on your candle and sprinkle it with your preferred oil/s. Light the candle. Focus on the candlelight and look at the image on the Tarot card (or you may prefer to use an image you have found in a magazine of the type of person you are seeking to attract) and say the following words nine times while you are focusing your will on the image bathed with the light of the candle:

"May this spell work for the benefit of all concerned."

Depending on how practiced you are, sit focusing on the image until just before you feel too tired. Place the candle in a bowl of sand in a tiled area of your home. If you put it in the bath tub or sink, make sure that a plug is covering the hole.

Potions

Potions have been made from time immemorial to attract the desired lover and to inflame sexual relationships. These potions were often made to be taken internally, and usually included warming substances, such as cloves, cinnamon and rose geranium.

The most famous of all aphrodisiac herbs is the satyrion root which was mentioned in ancient times as a common erotic aid. Although the root has never been botanically matched to a modern equivalent, the root of an orchid is often called satyrion root. Other roots, such as the root of ginseng and that of St John's wort (colorfully known as "John the Conqueror") have also been symbols of fertility. Other ingredients in love potions turned out to be nothing more than poisons, which served to irritate the taker who would mistake the effects of slight poisoning with renewed sexual vigor.

Some love potions were designed so that after the brew was taken the first person whom the drinker saw would be their intended partner for life. Others would inspire vivid dreams in which the drinker would see their true beloved. It is possible that these types of potions open the drinker's psychic abilities, allowing them to tap into their own intuition which allows the drinker to see the person they know deep inside is really the right mate for them.

In order to spread its potency around you, another type of love potion is the one that can be brewed and decanted into an ornamental bottle which may then be hung around your neck with a chain long enough to allow the bottle to reach your heart.

If you want to attract a friend or lover who has a balanced nature and can provide a stable relationship, try combining ingredients that reflect all the four elements of air, fire, water and earth. If you seek to communicate clearly with others, focus on the element of air. If you seek to forgive past grievances, invoke the element of water. If you seek to ignite passion or inspiration and to find a sense of joy in your sexuality or creativity, focus on the element of fire. If you wish to enhance the sense of dependability, invoke the element of earth.

Using the following chart, pick your ingredients from each element and combine them into a potion. If your mixture is too dry, use a quantity of almond oil so that you can decant your potion into the bottle. Almonds were traditionally believed to help find a love that will withstand all trials and tribulations. The bottle should be thoroughly cleansed by running water and dried in moonlight. As you make your mixture, focus on what you really want to achieve, projecting those thoughts into the bottle and corking it when finished. You may then wish to seal the bottle with a bit of red candle wax and place it in a safe place, possibly in a drawer beside your bed.

Air	Fire	Water	Earth
2 orange blossoms	2 jasmine flower petals	2 rose petals	2 lavender stalks
2 drops lemon essential oil	2 drops ylang-ylang essential oil	2 drops geranium essential oil	2 drops patchouli essential oil
2 teaspoons vodka	2 teaspoons whisky	2 teaspoons gin	2 teaspoons brandy
ginger	ginseng	parsley	garlic
cloves	sweet paprika	cinnamon	nutmeg

You may incorporate into your potion any other waterproof object of significance to your wish. Notice that most of the ingredients come in twos. This is an important number to focus on in love magic. You may also incorporate other traditional ingredients, such as dog hair, in your potion or spells. All you need is two strands from your pet. Dogs have been a symbol of faithfulness for many centuries, often included in old family portraits to show that the wife and/or husband are true to one another.

A loving cup full

For a love potion cordial that you may drink for love magic purposes, try Parfait Amor, a liquor which is citrus based and flavored with essence of violets.

Charms

Charms are magical words, chants or prayers that have been used through the ages to attract a loved one. However, merely reciting a charm is not enough — you would also have to enfold its power in an object which would then be wrapped in linen and placed under the front door of the person you desire. Once the person steps over the charm, its power comes alive and does your bidding.

Again this type of charm could be seen as overly manipulative and should be avoided as it tampers with the free will of another person. But there are many powerful charms that can bring your true lover to you or will help you see who is your true lover or friend.

Folklore is a huge source of charms and verses that have been handed down, the origin often obscured over many centuries and sometimes with variations that have replaced the original words. Despite this, often the intent and use of those words over generations for a particular purpose have imbued even nonsensical words with power. For example, magic squares have been used to attract love. Write the following square on a piece of white paper. Gaze upon the square and think of attracting love and friendship to yourself. Cut the square out and carry it with you for three days and three nights, then burn it. Watch the smoke mix with the air as it carries your message through the ether.

Magic square

S	A	T	O	R
A	R	E	P	O
T	E	N	E	T
O	P	E	R	A
R	O	T	A	S

Charms can be natural objects, such as acorns, which were believed to make an unfaithful lover repentant. Charms can also be written down on wood and worn around the neck in a decorative container or as an amulet. If you have a decorative container that you can wear as a necklace, you may consider making a charm with the following simple words written on a piece of wood.

Let me and thee
Most happy be.

Balsa or other light fibrous wood is perfect for marking with a ball point pen. You may include part of a bay leaf, lemon balm or heart's ease to attract love and romance to you. To enhance the power of your necklace further, consecrate it to the four elements. To consecrate means to dedicate the purpose of the object to your desire. You can do this by sprinkling the necklace or other charm with salted water (water), passing it over a flame (fire) and incense smoke (air) and then sprinkling earth over it (earth).

Traditional spellcraft
A moonstone bathed with the light of the
waxing moon can be charged with your
wish for a true lover. However, the charm
will only last until the next full moon.

51

Dream magic

Dreams are thought to be part of the world of the unconscious mind. When dreaming, the unconscious mind has access to all your fears, desires and inhibitions, and randomly weaves dreams that show you pictures, sounds, feelings and scents. It is believed that dreams give us important information about ourselves and those close to us.

Often dreams are about conflicts, and by focusing on your dreams over a period of time, you will find that your dreams may be offering solutions about any troublesome relationships you are experiencing. Place a sprig of rosemary or thyme under your pillow to make sure that you will not have nightmares.

Buy a good sized journal and keep a record of the dreams you have, particularly if you are experiencing an unhappy or lonely time. After a week, reread your entries and see if a consistent theme is emerging. Learn from your dreams.

You can also encourage your dreams to give you information on a specific topic. Traditionally, charms were devised to help the sleeper discover the identity of their future lover. For example, recite the following charm three times just before you fall asleep and see if you get a sign of who your lover will be:

Good St. Thomas, do me right
And bring my love to me this night
That I do look him in the face
And in my arms may him embrace

Alternatively, if you feel that this charm is too much of a mouthful, try placing a four-leafed clover or a symbol of a four-leafed clover under your pillow before you go to sleep. It is thought that you will dream of your soul mate.

Dream magic is best practiced during a full moon. If you seek information about a new love or friend, you can use the light of the full moon to cleanse your pillows of any previous negative energies before you dedicate your night's dreaming to your purpose. Air your pillows and fluff them in the light of the full moon.

Write down your question for your unconscious. Allow yourself to focus on your purpose. Leave your journal open and go to sleep. You must keep in mind that the unconscious often presents solutions or situations in symbols. The full meaning of symbols cannot usually be learnt from a dictionary of dream symbols — you have your own unique vocabulary of symbols. After working with your dreams for a while, you will find that you begin to understand your dreams and yourself very much better.

Herb Lore

Write your love wish on a sage leaf and put it under your pillow for three nights. If you dream of your love wish, then it will come true.

Magical ethics

The spells, charms and other techniques in love magic are beneficial in nature. It is important to remember the traditional law of Western magic: "If it harm none, do what you will." You must be careful when deciding what spell to cast that you do not act selfishly or try to hurt anyone. The danger in such practices are akin to the Eastern concept of karma, that whatever is sent out returns in time upon the sender. In Western magic, the formula is said to be "that which is sent out returns threefold."

Sometimes it is legitimate that a spell is worked to bind someone from doing harm to others. White witches have been known to work such magic when it is perceived to be for the greater good. However, there is always a price to be paid.

As you have seen, to achieve a successful result through your spellcraft, it is important to focus clearly on the outcome you want. But you also need to give yourself the time to think through the consequences of the spell.

It is advisable, unless in dire circumstances, always to ask the permission of the person involved before casting any spell, since otherwise the recipient of your best intentions may feel that their privacy has been invaded. Love spells should be approached with particular caution. It is fine to ask for a glimpse at one's future lover, but it is not ethical to make someone fall in love with you or anyone else using spellcraft. This can be categorized as black magic because you are tampering with a person's free will.

With love potions, please be careful to make them for yourself only, or if you wish to share the gift with someone, let them know and get their permission — you are wasting a lot of energy if the person is not interested. This is possibly one reason why past magicians needed to call up spirits of the dead to coerce the desired person into showing the right amount of interest. However, the magician usually had to pay a heavy price — these spirits tended to charge quite heavily for their services.

Heart-shaped amulets were worn originally to prevent the soul from leaving the body on the command of an unscrupulous magician.

Strengthening Your Relationships

Bringing back the romance in your life

Any strong long-term relationship has its share of ups and downs. Sometimes the problems stem from taking each other for granted. Love magic teaches a high level of respect for nature, yourself and those around you. This form of magic is not a band-aid solution. To strengthen your relationship/s you must be fully committed to respecting the people that are close to you, particularly since magic is all about learning to focus your will. If you feel that you and your partner have grown apart through pressures of work or any other issues, consider revising what is important to you. Work out your priorities. A good exercise is to visualize yourself at the end of your life, looking back at what you have done. Do you have any regrets? Are you surrounded by loving people, wishing only the best for you? Do you feel that you behaved with integrity in your dealings with your loved ones?

If you are dogged by heavy work pressure, try scheduling a date with your partner or friends, making time at least once a week to do something that will help bond you together. Sharing a meal is a lovely way to strengthen trust (see also page 21). Traditionally, the sharing of bread symbolized a bonding between loved ones.

If you are cooking the meal, make it extra special by focusing on an image of a loving and caring relationship while preparing the food. If both of you are comfortable in the kitchen, see if each of you can focus your love and caring into the food you are preparing.

The act of planning, digging and planting a love garden dedicated to your love together is also an exceptionally powerful bonding activity. By dedicating a special section of your garden to love, you are creating a profound sense of earth magic and, by tending to your garden, you remind yourself to tend to your loved ones as well.

Your love garden can be as large or as small as you want. Traditionally, a heart- or diamond-shaped section of land should be staked out. If you only have a courtyard, purchase or recycle a tub that can be put aside for your love garden. Edge your tub or selected plot with chamomile or pennyroyal and plant white flowers amid silvery gray foliage. This is also in honor of the moon, symbolizing the goddess element in nature. Also use plants in your love garden that are appropriately named, such as love-in-the-mist or the Kiss of Desire rose.

In feng shui, a particular section of the house represents relationships. If your house is irregularly shaped, square off the shape and see whether there is an empty space near the back of the house on the right hand side. According to the bagua (see page 26), this is the relationship sector. Plant or place a potted fruiting tree on the missing right hand corner to strengthen that sector. You may also consider planting a love garden within the missing section of the house.

(see page 26)

Planting marigolds

It is believed in some Slavic countries that if you plant marigolds in the earth scooped up from the footprint of the person you love, their love for you will last while the flowers are in bloom.

The value of respect and goodwill

I love thee to the depth and breadth and height my soul can reach.
Elizabeth Barrett Browning

A sense of generosity or goodwill is an exceptionally important aspect of a happy and long-lasting relationship. Expressing respect and goodwill helps those you love to open their souls to you.

The successful incorporation of goodwill and respect in a relationship in which such aspects have been lost requires all three of the following characteristics:

- the ability to give unconditionally and happily
- the insight to understand and balance the needs of yourself and your friend or partner
- the strength to keep true to yourself.

You may consider using moon magic to help yourself acquire or regain these characteristics. In Western magic, the moon has three aspects, called the Maid, Mother and the Crone, corresponding with the new, full and waning moons. The Maid is able to give unconditionally and happily without sense of hurt or fear. The Mother is more experienced and knowledgeable about the ways of the world, while the Crone is aware fully of who she is and the extent of her powers.

You can tailor these characteristics to suit your particular situation by performing a simple meditation in your special space on one of these aspects of the moon. For instance, to focus on the Maid and her ability to give freely, choose to do your meditation at new moon. Focus on your relationship and, if you are able to see the new moon from the window of your special space, focus also on the moon. Breathe normally, allowing the thoughts to flow through your head. Those to do with everyday matters, such as the shopping list, allow to flow away. Thoughts that are pertinent to your issue, allow to dwell in your mind. You may receive a series of insights.

When you feel ready, come back to full consciousness and write your insights in your journal. In honor of the moon, make sure that you make an effort to incorporate her insights into your life. Do not be careless with the power of the moon. Remember that respecting yourself, your loved ones and nature is a powerful aspect of love magic and lends success to the strength of your spells and wishes.

Consider giving your lover or friend a wish box. Purchase or make a simple box and decorate it according to your taste. Put three bay leaves in the box, a piece of parchment paper and a new pen for your friend or lover to make a wish, or insert a particular wish for him or her.

Learning to listen

Familiar acts are beautiful through love
Percy Bysshe Shelley

The ability to listen and to draw conclusions from your feelings allows
you to develop a richer and stronger appreciation of the way in which the
world works, your role in it and the feelings of your loved one. Fears,
such as the fear of being inadequate, get in the way of listening properly.
Remember that we are perpetual students of life — there is always
something new that can be learned. In intimate or troubled relationships,
the sheer act of listening can go a long way toward healing any rifts.

The first step is to set aside some time in the evening or on the
weekend. Give a generous amount of time to your friend or lover,
allowing for any difficulties getting started. The second step is to consider
sharing your special space or, preferably, creating a different special
space for the two of you. Think about furnishing your new space with
either two comfortable chairs facing each other or a number of cushions
and pillows. Decorate your friend's or lover's chair or cushions with
predominantly blue fabric. Decorate your side with green fabric. Blue
resonates to the throat chakra while green resonates to the heart chakra.

A potion to help communication

Many kinds of fears can get in the way of communication.
Try five drops of the following Bach Flower Remedies
directly under your tongue:

- *Beech for feelings of intolerance*
- *Larch if you lack confidence in yourself*
- *Impatiens if you feel impatient or irritable.*

Dr. Edward Bach developed thirty-eight remedies extracted from
various flowers of wild plants, bushes and trees, which help
alleviate negative states of mind.

You may choose to make your friend more comfortable in the space by casting a blue light around the immediate area or by sitting close enough so that you are both able to place a hand over the other's heart. If your friend or lover is too emotional to talk, sit in this position and focus on his or her heart or any other area that symbolizes the emotions to you. To help with your heart connection, use a drop of rose oil and rub it on your heart chakra.

When you both feel ready, stop or have a break. Have a thermos of a hot drink handy and something sweet, like some quality chocolates or biscuits. Again, this is the concept of the breaking of bread together that enhances an often subconscious feeling of trust. Always end this session with a long hug. Sincere hugs are now well known for their therapeutic qualities.

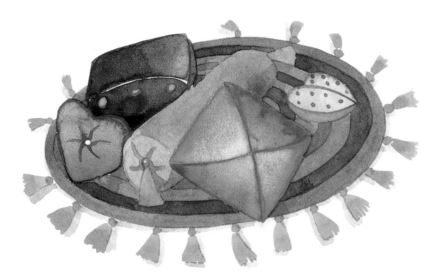

Trust and sharing

To practice love magic, you must be able to trust in yourself. Extending the trust to those you love is a way of sharing that magic. You may wish to perform the following meditation to strengthen your feelings of trust in other people.

Sit or lie down comfortably in your special space. Concentrate on your breathing, drawing in a feeling of calmness, and exhaling the tensions of the everyday. As you begin to feel a sense of serenity, visualize a circle of blue light around your space. Close your eyes and visualize the circle growing into a sphere of blue light. Make the circle as big as you wish.

Imagine carving a doorway in the sphere and sending an invitation to those you love to join you in your circle. Imagine the various people coming into your space, standing along the perimeter of your circle. Many you will recognize; however, do not be surprised if there are some people you do not know — they may well be one of your ancestors, a spirit guide, or your intuition's image of a future love. When you feel that there are enough people standing around the edge of your circle, close the door.

Allow the feeling of their love and trust to emanate in waves toward you. Imagine the waves being powerful enough to raise you bodily from where you are sitting or lying. You may at this stage actually feel like standing up to feel the warmth and delight of the acceptance being sent to you. Breathe in the feeling. Swim in it.

Then, imagine a chalice filled with nectar. Watch it being passed from soul to soul, each taking a sip and giving the chalice a blessing. Visualize the chalice being handed to you. Drink the nectar, feeling the blessings and nurture from the souls invited by your unconscious. Imagine leaving only a few drops in the chalice, which you then pour back into the earth, honoring the earth and grounding into it the energy you have raised.

As the drops soak into the earth, imagine your visitors blending into the blue sphere, and allow the blue light to become absorbed within your body, before traveling down into your feet and through into the ground. Concentrate on your breathing again. Wriggle your fingers and toes and allow your body a huge stretch. Carry with you the sense of trust and nurture that your visitors have bestowed upon you.

Sharing the joy of awakening your senses together

You can explore the sensations of sharing and trusting another person by each of you attuning your senses to the other. Take turns to share the experiences of smell, hearing, taste, touch and sight together. Gather all your favorite scents, special food and soft textured material, feathers or scarves. Blindfold your partner. Present him or her with one or two of your favorite scents or essential oils. Give your partner time to breathe in the scent. To explore the sensation of hearing, you may use a small pair of Tibetan gongs, which make a lovely delicate sound, or a crystal glass. Next, feed your lover with something tasty, perhaps good quality chocolates. For touch, glide feathers, scarves and silks around your lover's face and body. For sight, untie the blindfold and take some time to gaze into each other's eyes, taking the time to fully appreciate the inner beauty of your loved one.

Deepening the intimacy

Every day, every hour, every moment makes me feel more deeply
how blessed we are in each other.
William Wordsworth

A strong sense of intimacy can come from sharing in each other's spirituality. The easiest way of doing this is to share your dreams. Study each other's use of symbols and images. Sometimes, you might find that you share a common image or even an entire dream.

There are groups of people who have bonded strongly because each one shares an image of the same event, such as a battle, or place, such as a monastery, in their dreams. Occasionally, it is enough that you both experience the same type of dream, such as being pursued by an unknown predator. Explore each other's dreams and help each other to obtain a deeper sense of meaning in them.

There are other methods of spiritual connection. With your lover, you may wish to sit quietly to deepen your sense of spiritual connection before making love. Sit with your legs entwined and knees bent, facing each other. Visualize a ribbon of light connecting both of you at each chakra point. Allow the light to be appropriately colored to correspond with each chakra (see pages 16–17). Imagine both your chakras lit and pulsing.

Each of you should then imagine that a golden light is running up from the ground through your spine to the top of your head, connecting the chakras. Allow the golden light to spray up through the top of your head and come back down to the ground along the sides of your arms. This symbolizes your balance between sharing your energy and staying strong within yourself.

You may also consider making a little pouch of leather or silk to hold a token of your lover or

> **Here is a list of things you can try to deepen your sense of intimacy with your lover:**
> - *with closed eyes, gently stroke and caress each other's face;*
> - *wash each other's hair, feet or whole body;*
> - *feed each other; and*
> - *lie in each other's arms quietly, listening to each other's heartbeat.*

64

friend. This is particularly potent magic if you have to be apart from each other for any length of time. The amulet can hold a lock of your loved one's hair, their favorite stone or herb. Think about including part of a sprig of rosemary, to enhance the happy memories you have had with your loved one. If your loved one favors a particular perfume or aftershave, dab a touch of it on the amulet before you close the pouch.

Thread a leather thong or silk cord through the top of the pouch and wear your amulet close to your heart. As a gift to a loved one going on a journey that they do not feel comfortable about, make an amulet of a lock of your own hair and include a calming herb such as lavender. Before you cut your hair for the amulet, concentrate on feeling supportive and comforting to your loved one during the trip. This will dedicate the amulet to its purpose.

Saying Goodbye

Saying goodbye with dignity and strength

There are a number of healing rituals that can be done to help say goodbye to someone you have cared for. You may have lost someone very dear to you through a growing apart in a relationship or through death.

Where you are suffering the irrevocable breakdown of a relationship, consider performing a simple ceremony. Gather together a photograph of the person, a few sprigs of rosemary, a candle and some earth or sand in a bowl or a cauldron. Choose a candle of a color that you feel resonates with the person you have parted from and anoint it with a fragrance that reminds you of him or her, whether it is an essential oil or a drop or two of his or her favorite perfume or aftershave. Inscribe the person's name along the side of the candle, dedicating the candle to his or her remembrance.

Secure the candle into the bowl or cauldron of earth or sand and arrange the sprigs of rosemary around the bottom of the candle. You may wish to set up your prepared candle and the photograph in your special space. Allow yourself a full evening for this ritual.

Light the candle and give a small prayer of thanks for having met your friend or lover. Even the most negative of relationships have taught you some lesson. While gazing into the candlelight, meditate on your friend or lover, wishing him or her well in his or her new life. Remain in this meditative state for as long as you feel comfortable. Once the meditation ends, you can leave your candle to burn down in its bowl or cauldron and allow the smoke to rise up with all your good wishes. If you feel it appropriate, repeat this ceremony for three nights, allowing yourself as much time as you need to heal the break of your bonds with this other person.

This ceremony may help you move onto the next phase of your life. Even if you are pleased with the breakup, consider doing a goodbye ceremony. It is an appropriate way of honoring the person who has passed through your life. By honoring him or her you are also honoring yourself, and you may receive some interesting insights concerning the relationship that will help you build better and stronger ones in the future.

This is also a satisfying ceremony to perform when we have lost someone through death. Often when someone we love dies, we find that we have not had the time or warning that we needed to say goodbye and let that person know how much we really cared for them. Even if there were many difficulties in the relationship, there is a point where death sometimes gives us a perspective of the soul of that person, and we mourn the loss. No matter how tragic a passing, there must be a time for the celebration of and thanksgiving for the life that preceded it.

A helpful potion

Consider taking the following essential flower essences to help relieve the pain of your loss:

Rock rose — *to relieve panic*
Star of Bethlehem — *to relieve shock*
Impatiens — *to relieve stress*
Cherry plum — *to relieve a sense of desperation*
Clematis — *to help you feel anchored back in reality.*

These essences have been commercially blended and are called, among other names, "Rescue Remedy" or "Emergency Essence".

Dealing with loss

When dealing with the loss of a loved one through death or the ending of a relationship, we are in effect passing through a rite of passage. You may feel the sadness of the loss or you may be battling an almost overwhelming sense of anger, grief or injustice. Sadness resonates with the element of water, symbolized by tears. Anger, grief or injustice resonates with the element of fire.

Allow yourself a three-day ceremony to help mark the passing or loss of your loved one. On the first day, you may wish to do a goodbye ceremony, honoring the person you have lost (see pages 66–67). On the second day, consider commemorating your sadness about the loss through another small ceremony at night.

Bring to your special space a chalice, filled with a drink that you may have shared with your loved one sometime in the past. If you are burning a second remembrance candle, focus on the candle and allow yourself to feel the sadness rising within.

Save one tear drop and mix it with your drink. Take two sips only, giving a blessing to your loved one and another to the feelings that you are experiencing. When you are ready, take your chalice outside and present it to the moon, perhaps catching the moon's beams or image on the surface of your drink. Pour the rest of the liquid in the chalice into the earth, imagining your sadness mingling with the power of the earth. Imagine that sense of power flowing into you giving you a sense of renewal.

On the third day, consider working with your feelings of grief, anger or injustice. Often these emotions stem from a feeling of helplessness because we know that we cannot change what has happened. As you burn your third candle of remembrance, visualize the flame of the candle as part of an ancient fire that has been burning throughout all time. Visualize feeding the flame with all your feelings of grief, anger or injustice. Imagine the flame rising higher until it engulfs the world, cleansing it and purifying it. Visualize the flame becoming a deep, glowing light, illuminating your loved one's path and helping him or her follow his or her new direction.

Ancient Wisdom
Instead of averting your eyes from the painful events of life, look at them squarely and contemplate them often. By facing the realities of death, infirmity, loss and disappointment, you free yourself of illusions and false hopes and you avoid miserable, envious thoughts.
Epictetus, *The Art of Living*, 55 A.D.—135 A.D.

Envy, jealousy and obsession

Love is like quicksilver in the hand. Leave the fingers open and it stays.
Clutch it, and it darts away.
Dorothy Parker

Jealousy and envy are two of the most debilitating emotions in human relations and can eat away at a person's soul. If you are suffering from these emotions yourself, consider writing in a journal where you feel these emotions are stemming from.

Often jealousy and envy come from a feeling of powerlessness, of being unable to carve out a unique and favorable position for yourself or find the right partner or friend. Consider following a number of the exercises from pages 32–45 to strengthen your feelings of power and attractiveness.

We all have a unique destiny that manifests desirable results at different times. We must never be jealous or envious of another person because, apart from anything else, we can never have any full conception of exactly what sacrifices and pains that other person has had to endure to get to that certain point in his or her life.

Obsession also stems from a feeling of powerlessness. If you are suffering from feeling obsessed with another person, take some time to focus on what exactly it is about that person that obsesses you. Write down a list. You may also have a feeling that the person is perhaps "dangerous" for you. There could be an element of excitement that may be unlocking something within your soul. It could be a clue from your unconscious telling you that you need to make some changes.

Understand what qualities that person represents to you and consider implementing some, if not all, of those qualities into your life. For example, your person may trigger in you a feeling of exotic places, travel and new experiences. Try to implement a travel plan for yourself and shake up your routine. Even just imagine changing your lifestyle. Now look at the person you've desired again — has the attraction lessened?

Sometimes people feel that a spell has been cast to make them love a person obsessively. In reality, there are few people who can truly pull off such a spell. However, a person close to you may be, often unintentionally, projecting intense feelings of envy or jealousy. There are two very good ways of sealing yourself off from such emotions.

First, you may wish to seal all the windows of your house, particularly in the space where you dream. In front of each window, make the sign of the pentacle (see diagram) and sprinkle some salt water around each window as well as any doors leading to the outside world. For intimate protection, consider anointing each opening in your body with salted water, imagining that you are blocking all such negative energy from entering your body.

Coping with rejection

The feeling of rejection is one of the most unhappy feelings a person can experience. However, keep in mind that by allowing yourself to feel unwanted and unloved after a rejection, you are effectively giving your personal power away. After the initial shock or feelings of sadness, try some of the exercises in pages 32–45 to help your feelings of self-worth and give you the strength to re-emerge.

If you seek something more, consider visiting the Crone, one of the triple goddesses of the moon (the others being the Maid and the Mother). She is the wise woman and represents the dark time of the moon, helping those in their darkest hour grasp a stronger sense of their self. You can access her wisdom by doing a meditation, preferably during the time of the waning moon.

Sit or lie down in a comfortable space and concentrate on your breathing. Allow your body to relax and your mind to let go of everyday concerns. Imagine that you are on a path leading away from a village. The village represents the everyday world. As you walk along the path, you move deeper and deeper into a dark forest. Despite the darkness, you are not afraid. You continue on your path until you see ahead a small clearing and the pathway leading to an old gnarled oak door with strong iron hinges. Knock on the door and feel that you are invited to enter.

As you enter the cottage, you feel a sense of deep acceptance and welcome. Emerging from the dark, the Crone greets you. She can take the image of any older person you have liked or admired or you may feel that she is an older version of yourself. Whichever image you chose, you feel respect in her welcome.

Imagine two chairs facing each other beside a fireplace, so that as you sit down with the Crone, you are sitting almost knee to knee. Imagine gazing into her eyes and allow your mind to take in any insights she may give you or the answers to any questions you may have. Allow yourself as much time as possible in the Crone's comforting presence.

When you are ready, offer your thanks to the Crone, perhaps visualizing a small gift as a token of thanks. Gaze into the fire and imagine yourself walking through the dark forest toward a light. Count out nine steps, which bring you closer and closer to the light and full consciousness. Remember to write down the insights you have been given and allow yourself to feel the deep power of the Crone within you.

Protection against unwanted attention
— learning to say "no"

The first step to being able to say "no" in emotional situations is to believe in your own inner strength. There are two very successful magical techniques that can help you lock into your mind a vision of your strength.

The first involves finding a picture that epitomizes the type of strength you need. The picture could be of an animal, for instance, a hawk which is the symbol of vision and prophesy, or it could be of a person whom you deeply admire. Concentrate on the type of strength you need and allow your mind to play with any related thoughts and inspirations that may come to it while you are focusing on the issue. Write down any insights you have and, if they appear valid, begin implementing them in your life.

The second technique involves devising an affirmation that you can repeat each day to affirm your sense of personal power and strength. The actual wording of an affirmation is very important. The strength or change that you want to achieve can be worded as either an ongoing process, such as "I am feeling stronger each day", or as a foregone conclusion, such as "I am strong and well loved". Ideally try both techniques together to help you believe in your strength (see also pages 76–77).

The next step is to do a form of visualization that will help protect you in time of personal crisis and to avert unwanted attention. The visualization is like a cloak of invisibility. Imagine a blue circle of light shining around your body. Visualize this line expanding into a thick fuzzy sheet of blue light that envelops you in a soft cocoon. Once enveloped into this safe space, you are still able to move about; however, people may find it hard to focus on you clearly, giving you an opportunity to move out of the range of the unwanted attention.

When you are feeling safe, remember to earth the blue cocoon into the ground by sweeping your arms up to the top of your cocoon and "collecting" the light into your hands. Bring your hands down to the ground and visualize the energy running safely into the ground.

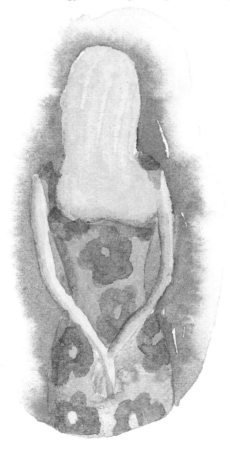

Love Magic Affirmations

The biggest danger in life is missing out on the promise
of life by avoiding the issues and retreating in fear.
Ashley Montague

Affirmations are the verbal equivalent of visualizations. You can use these affirmations instead of or to supplement a visualization during your meditations in your special space. The following affirmations are useful for common unhappy feelings in a relationship.

You can use these affirmations as a form of a mantra, where you repeat the sentence again and again. This is particularly useful when you are in a particularly deep state of relaxation. The mind is then ready to accept new information. Of course, if you do use one of the following affirmations or one of your own, make an effort to make what you say happen in the everyday world. The affirmations will only help you focus for a change, so generally you will need more than just the words to get the desired effect.

You may use any of the affirmations below or make up some of your own. It is important that the wording of the affirmation is positive. Use words that conjure an image of yourself successfully changing a troublesome feeling or having succeeded already.

Consider taking three drops of one of the following Dr. Bach's flower essences before saying the affirmation.

1. *I can be who I want to be and learn to balance the needs of others with my own.* To combat the feeling of being at other people's beck and call. Take three drops of Centaury before saying the affirmation.

2. *I receive all the love and happiness that I could really want.*

To combat feelings of possessiveness. Take three drops of Chicory before saying the affirmation.

3. *I feel secure in being loved for myself.*

To combat feeling overcritical of others. Take three drops of Chicory before saying the affirmation.

4. *I have the power to love and be loved.*

To combat the feeling of loneliness. Take three drops of Heather before saying the affirmation.

5. *I have the power to get all the love I need and all the love I want.*

To combat feelings of jealousy and envy. Take three drops of Holly before saying the affirmation.

6. *I am free to make mistakes and learn from them.*

To combat feelings of irritation at your mistakes. Take three drops of Impatiens before saying the affirmation.

7. *I am confident in what I say and in what I do.*

To combat the fear of people. Take three drops of Mimulus before saying the affirmation.

8. *Everything happens for a purpose.*

To combat feelings of guilt. Take three drops of Pine before saying the affirmation.

9. *I can love others for who they are.*

To combat feelings of being superior or overbearing. Take three drops of Vine before saying the affirmation.

10. *I am free from the actions of others who seek to harm me.*
To combat feelings of bitterness and anger. Take three drops of Willow before saying the affirmation.

Although Dr. Bach's flower essences are available in many countries, flower essences specific to certain countries have emerged. In the United States there are a number of distinctive flower essences available, including FES Quintessentials, the Flower Essences Services in Nevada City, California. In Australia, you may like to try Bush Flower Essences.

Your New Path

Love magic can be an enormously powerful form of magic. It is important to follow a particular path in introducing love magic into your life. First and foremost it is essential that you learn to nurture yourself, understanding the beauty and the balances involved in your life. Learn to respect yourself and live accordingly. Your capacity to give and receive love is the most powerful resource you have.

To help you understand yourself, learn to listen to the earth. Pay attention to the elements. Nature provides many examples of how the world works. Human beings have, through the ages, attempted to conquer nature rather than learn from her, often meeting with brief unsatisfying success or utter failure. Humans cannot escape totally the workings of nature.

Finally, work through those love magic exercises concerning your friends and lover that appeal to you. Enjoy the pleasure of giving while cultivating a sense of psychic balance. Enjoy rekindling relationships and finding new ones that nurture your individuality and strengths. Find a spiritual bonding with those you can call your family, both in reality and magically.

Love magic is designed to empower you and your loved ones to enjoy life to the fullest. May you find much happiness in seeking to love with all your heart.

Ancient Wisdom
Content yourself with being a lover of wisdom, a seeker of the truth.
Return and return again to what is essential and worthy.
Epictetus, *The Art of Living* (55 A.D. — 135 A.D.)

Glossary

Amulet — a protective device worn around the neck or hung from the door or window of a sacred space or home.

Ayurveda — a traditional system of medicine which originated in India over 5,000 years ago.

Bagua — in feng shui, a grid formula used to identify the different areas of the house that corresponds with aspects of the occupant's life.

Chakra — one of the seven major psychic energy centers running through the middle of the body. These chakra centers follow the same path as the spine, starting at the base of the spine and ending at the top of the head.

Chalice — or cup, one of the elemental tools symbolizing water and the emotions.

Charm — a magical word or words that can be used as a protection.

Circle — a sacred space, usually thought of as a sphere of energy created when the circle is cast.

Deosil — moving sunwise (clockwise in the Northern Hemisphere and counter-clockwise in the Southern Hemisphere).

Feng shui — a traditional system of balance, placement and design which originated in China.

Grounding — a term referring to connecting the body's energy with that of the earth.

Invoke — to summon a spirit or energy form into oneself.

Pentacle — a five-pointed star that symbolizes the four elements and the spirit. A metal version of this symbol can be worn as a protection. If the pentacle is upright, with the point uppermost, the pentacle is a symbol of love magic. If it is upside down, with the point at the bottom, the pentacle is a symbol of Satanism.

Scrying — a form of divination using reflective surfaces, such as a crystal ball, or smoke from a fire.

Talisman — an object charged to attract a specific magical energy.

Triple goddess — is the embodiment of female energy through the three states of womanhood, the Maid (virgin), the Mother and the Crone. These states are related to phases of the moon, i.e. the Maid correlates with the energy of the new moon, while the Mother relates to the energy of the full moon and the Crone equates with the energy of the dark or waning moon.

This edition published by Barnes & Noble, Inc.,
by arrangement with Lansdowne Publishing

1999 Barnes & Noble Books

M 10 9 8 7 6 5 4 3 2 1

ISBN 0-7607-1713-3

Published by Lansdowne Publishing Pty Ltd
Sydney NSW 2000, Australia

Text: Antonia Beattie
Designer: Sylvie Abecassis
Editor: Cynthia Blanche
Cover illustration: Penny Lovelock
Illustrator: Sue Ninham

Set in Cochin on QuarkXPress
Printed in China by Everbest Co. Ltd

Quotes from Epictetus are taken from a new interpretation by Sharon Lebell of
Epictetus works in *The Art of Living: The Classic Manual on Virtue, Happiness, and
Effectiveness*, published by HarperSan Francisco, 1995.

NOTE: You will notice that the start and finishing dates attributed to each star
sign vary slightly in the literature on astrology. Each sign gets to shine for
approximately 30 days each year. As a result, it is left to each astrologer to determine which signs will gain the extra five days. For those born either day of the
cusp, read both signs and determine which best describes you for the purposes of
the book.